FERRARI TESTAROSSA

FERRARI TESTAROSSA

David Sparrow

This book is dedicated to my Godson Samuel Gough

Acknowledgements

No book such as this is the result of one person's effort. I must thank; Peter Frater at TKM Automotive Ltd; Alan Mapp at Maranello Concessionaires; and Martin Jones at Nigel Mansell Sports Cars, (all in the UK), for their help in providing cars and information; Marino Varengo at Ferrari Head Office in Maranello, Italy, for his most generous assistance in providing car and driver during my stay; models Juliette Richardson and Jade Bond; and Uli Hintner at Leica GB Ltd for his most welcome help. The photographs in this book were shot on Kodak/Kodachrome film. I prefer using the amateur stock to the professional, as it stands up better to non-refrigerated travel! The cameras were Leica R6s, which I find so reliable and a joy to work with, plus lenses ranging from 16 mm to 400 mm. The outfit is housed in a bag manufactured and specially adapted by Billingham in the UK.

Half title page
The symbol of the prancing horse that has been the pride of Italy since the late 1940s

Title page
With its deliciously balanced engine, the Testarossa feels fine cruising at 140 mph. Try speeds like that in either Britain or the United States, however, and you'll soon be taking the bus

Right
The unmistakeable wedge shape of the Testarossa. Pininfarina was able to work the body into one of the most distinctive and instantly recognisable cars of the 1980s

Published in 1992 by Osprey Publishing
Reprinted Autumn 1996

ISBN 1 85532 649 3

Edited by Tony Holmes
Page design by Jessica Caws
Printed in Hong Kong

For a catalogue of all books published by Osprey Automotive please write to:

The Marketing Department, Osprey Publishing, 2nd Floor, Unit 6, Spring Gardens, Tinworth Street, London SE11 5EH

Contents

Introduction – Enzo Ferrari & Fiat

Enzo Ferrari died at his home on 14 August 1988. His name has been immortalized by the world's most exciting sports and touring cars. With the possible exception of the even more exotic F40, the Ferrari Testarossa was the last of the great touring cars spawned from the pure racing pedigree of Maranello, and spawned when the man whose name it bears still owned the major share in the company.

With the death of Enzo Ferrari, his 50 per cent share went to Fiat, which thus owned 90 per cent of Italy's most prestigious car manufacturer. The remaining 10 per cent was owned by Enzo's son, Piero Lardi-Ferrari (it has often been reported that Pininfarina owned one per cent, but he has steadfastly denied this).

Fiat's manufacturing involvement with the firm from Modena goes back to 1965 when on 1 March it was announced that Fiat would be using the Dino engine in one of its next GT cars which was to be called rather appropriately the Fiat Dino. Ferrari were also using the Dino engine in the Dino 206, which was presented to the world at the Paris show in 1965, and in the formula 2 car, which in order to qualify with the regulations had to have an engine derived from a mass-produced unit.

Ferrari had neither the sales potential nor the facilities to quickly produce the 500 engines (and vehicles) required for homologation. Hence the deal with Fiat which, for the Turin show of 1966, unveiled the Fiat Dino – a Fiat with a Ferrari engine!

Ferrari's involvement with Fiat went back much further, in fact, to the end of World War 1. After being demobbed Enzo Ferrari approached Fiat for a job. He was turned down, a rejection which, on that cold winter's day, caused him to weep openly. It also started a determination to exact, if not revenge, then at the very least the acknowledgement that he was a 'force-majeure'. Fiat would be made to acknowledge him. Ferrari worked elsewhere in Turin and in his spare time he raced cars. In 1920 he came second in the Targa Florio, driivng an Alfa 4500. After the race he moved to Portello, where the Alfa Romeo factory was situated. He continued racing for Alfa Romeo and it was during this part of his career that he came by that now famous symbol of the prancing horse. After winning a race at the Circuito del Savio, at Ravenna, Ferrari met Count Enrico Baracca and later his mother the Countess Paolina, who suggested that her son's emblem, the prancing horse, would bring Ferrari good luck.

The horse was black, but characteristically Ferrari chose his own colour for the background – pale yellow, the colour of his home town, Modena. The emblem soon appeared on Ferrari's Alfa Romeos.

Enzo Ferrari knew that racing was not his ultimate forte – he was above all an organiser and motivator. He persuaded Alfa Romeo to give him a project for

Left

The evocative name of Ferrari, given to the company by its founder, Enzo Ferrari, who was born in February 1898 in Modena, northern Italy. Thought of as one of Italy's greatest sons, Ferrari was granted the title of Commendatore by the Italian Fascists. After World War 2, when Fascist honours were reviewed, the engineer happily reverted to just plain old Enzo Ferrari

which he was ideally suited; he was to find engineers for the Alfa Romeo factory in Milan. Ferrari relieved Fiat of Luigi Bazzi (who would work for Ferrari for the rest of his life) and also of Vittorio Jano, who went on to become a great designer. Ferrari's quest for revenge had begun.

Ferrari continued racing as he built up the Alfa Romeo team, often driving with Bazzi by his side. At this time, the team barnstormed the racing circuits. In 1924, Alfa's win in the French Grand Prix produced an unexpected offshoot. Fiat, trounced by Alfa, gave up racing. The migration of engineers from Turin to Milan had, no doubt, some bearing on this decision.

In 1929 Enzo Ferrari founded the Scuderia Ferrari and in 1932 this racing 'stable' took over the management of Alfa Romeo's racing division. The SCUDERIA modified cars from Alfa – always improving them – and then got its customers to race them! In this way, Ferrari developed a team with names of mythical proportion: Campari, Arcangeli, Varzi, Chiron, Fagioli, Nuvolari.

Aside from racing, Ferrari the businessman was also at work. His Alfas were not cheap and Ferrari gave nothing away. If you couldn't afford a Ferrari Alfa – then, quite simply, you didn't get one!

But, of all the Alfa Romeo projects Ferrari was involved with, the most notable was the creation of the 158 at Modena in 1937. It was designed by Gioacchino Colombo, conceived by Ferrari, and powered by a 150 cc supercharged engine. Four 158s were made and these cars, together with the later 159, were the pinnacle of Alfa Romeo's racing achievement.

By 1939 Ferrari was becoming disenchanted with Alfa Romeo. Like so many other innovative people, he became bored quickly. He thrived on technical problems and needed a smooth running team to produce results. But the arrival at Alfa Romeo of the designer Ricart put paid to that.

Ferrari and Ricart just could not work together, and this clash of personalities provided the necessary impetus for Ferrari to go it alone.

After 20 years at Alfa Romeo, Ferrari founded AUTO AVIO CONSTUZIONI (Auto Aviation Construction). He took with him his friend Bazzi, who had been harshly treated by Ricart.

Because of the terms of his contract with Alfa Romeo, Ferrari was not to put his name on a racing car for four years and so it was that AAC's first project was to build a racing car for the 1940 Mille Miglia. Built from parts made at AAC in the Scuderia buildings, and other parts bought from Fiat (that link again!) the car had an eight cylinder engine of 1500 cc and was known simply as 815. Two were built, and then driven by Ascari and Macchiavelli – both failed to finish. Both cars have disappeared now. Ferrari himself lost interest in them once the race was over and had no ideas of starting a museum!

The war put an end to racing, and AAC produced small aero engines of four cylinders, as well as petrol driven grinding machines. In 1943 the firm moved to Maranello while the Scuderia remained at Modena.

Things gradually go back to normal after the war and racing started again. Ferrari's obsession with 'the engine' was showing. During 1946 139 prototype

A range of Ferraris at Nigel Mansell Sports Cars. After leaving Alfa Romeo in 1929, Enzo Ferrari, along with the Caniato brothers, set up the Societa Anonima Scuderia Ferrari – an independent Alfa agency looking after Alfa's racing clients. It would be a further 17 years before he started to build cars with the Ferrari marque

The Testarossa's racing heritage is on display at the Mansell showrooms. Also on display is Mansell's own mount – a far cry from the Ferrari 815 of 1940

engines were built for the first car to carry the name Ferrari – the 125.

April 1947 saw the 125 project completed and tested. Two cars were entered for a race at Piacenza on 11 May, one driven by Franco Cortese and the other by Nino Farina (who crashed in practice damaging his car too badly to race). Cortese eased into the lead on the 21st lap and stayed there until his engine cut out (due to a broken fuel pump) on the 27th lap, at which point he was some 25 seconds ahead of Angiolini's Maserati.

On 25 May Cortese's car was entered in the Roman Grand Prix, and this time gained victory. The Ferrari had won at only the second attempt! In fact, during 1947 Ferrari entered his cars in 14 races, winning seven of them, and achieving four second places. An auspicious start!

During 1948, the number of races entered had increased to 28, of which Ferrari's took ten first places, eleven second places and six thirds. One of those ten first places was in the Mille Miglia. 1949 saw a second Mille Miglia win and a first place at Le Mans in the 24 hours race; Luigi Chinetti's Ferrari 2000 won with an average speed of 132.946 mph.

The win at Le Mans was of particular importance for Enzo Ferrari and his factory, for it proved that his cars were solid and reliable, as well as fast – an important consideration when you build touring road cars. Many wealthy connoisseurs were beginning to notice the prancing horse.

In 1950 Ferrari entered his team in 74 races. They won 46, came second in 33 and third in 18. The following year was the golden one for Ferrari. This was the year in which the great Alfa Romeo 159, the successor to the 158, was decisively beaten, Gonzales finishing in his Ferrari some 51 seconds ahead of Fangio's 159. 1951 also saw a fourth Ferrari win of the Mille Miglia.

In 1952 Ferrari won the Mille Miglia again, repeating its success in 1953 (and 1956 and 1957) and 1954 brought another win at Le Mans for what was becoming Italy's premier team.

One of the most momentous events in the Ferrari story came in 1955. With Alfa Romeo firmly out of the running, Ferrari looked more and more like the representative of Italian honour on the race-track. In July this was confirmed by the withdrawal of the Lancia team from racing.

Moreover Lancia handed over all of its racing equipment to Ferrari. Some have estimated the value of this gift at L1,000,000,000. As if that was not enough to get the champagne corks popping, Fiat, realising that with the demise of Lancia, Ferrari was indeed Italy's flag bearer, donated a sum of L250,000,000 payable at L50,000,000 per year over five years. This sense of national honour, shown by all three firms in this very special drama, was to be a major element in events a decade later.

1956 was another important year, as Ferrari launched a 2 litre, 4 cylinder roadster with the name Testa Rossa. The car was really rather unremarkable except for the camshaft covers which were painted red. The following year saw the development of the 250 Testa Rossa, with its red-headed 3 litre V12 and in 1958 this car dominated the World Championship, winning every round in which

Right
The prancing horse emblem originally belonged to World War I flying ace Francesco Baracca, who was killed in 1918 after shooting down 34 enemy aircraft. After several successes at the 1923 Circuit of Savio, Ferrari was personally congratulated by Francesco's father, Count Enrico Baracca

Left
Francesco's mother, the Countess Paolina Baracca, dedicated her son's coat of arms to Ferrari in order to bring him luck. Ferrari adopted it as his badge, putting the emblem on a golden shield in honour of Modena. The badge first appeared on Ferrari's racing Alfas

they competed with the exception of the race at the Nurbourgring.

At Le Mans, ten Testa Rossas took part winning in convincing style, and so it went on until Aston Martin put a stop to it in 1959. A change in regulations in 1962 brought success for the 250 GTO, which was simply a renamed Testa Rossa, as was the engine of the 250P which took Ferrari to the top of the prototypes in 1963.

Ferrari had proved themselves a force to be reckoned with in Formula 1, winning the World Championship in 1952 and 1953 with Ascari, and with Fangio in 1956. Two years later Mike Hawthorn won the title for Ferrari, but an interesting technical development had taken place. When the new season opened, Stirling Moss won the Argentinian Grand Prix with a rear-engined Cooper. Carlo Chiti, Ferrari's chief engineer (who left Alfa Romeo to join Ferrari), was so convinced that the rear-engined layout was the way ahead that he set to work on an experimental car.

Enzo Ferrari was livid. He maintained that the horse should 'pull the cart, not push it'. Chiti, however, persevered so that a rear-engined car was available for the next season. The rest, as they say, is history. Rear-engined cars have dominated Formula 1 ever since and it is certain that the choice of engine layout on the Dino project two years later was a direct result of this change.

It was at about this time that Ford approached Enzo Ferrari with a view to buying him out. Ford were keen to enter Le Mans, and what better way than by buying up an expert team?

Ferrari was keen to put his business on a long term, secure footing. Racing stables cost money and research and development put a severe strain on funds,

Ferrari's involvement with Alfa Romeo
brought them the world championship,
a fact that the Alfa Romeo museum at
Arese celebrates. Colombo's masterpiece,
the 158, is shown on the right

Engineer Ricart, the man responsible for
Ferrari and his colleague Luigi Bazzi
leaving the Alfa stable, developed the 159
– the car that Ferrari trounced in 1950

so the idea of a merger with a car giant was most attractive. But for Ferrari the nationalist, the patriot, was an American firm the proper 'home' for Italy's greatest racing stable? The talks with Ford did not go well.

Ferrari wanted to maintain control over the experimental racing side, but was happy to pass up the commercial sector. The Americans thought this unreasonable. A figure had been put to Ferrari, a level set in the States. Ferrari shrewdly asked a member of the negotiating team to what limit he could negotiate above that figure without first seeking authorisation. The reply was a shock $10,000, the cost of a Ferrari car! In the grand scheme of things, it seemed, Ferrari was not as important as he thought!

The outcome, however, was to get Fiat more and more interested, so that when the Ford deal fell through, Fiat stepped in. Thus Enzo Ferrari finally joined Fiat as an associate after being refused work 50 years before.

For their part Fiat kept in the background until the late 1970s when the Fiat sign appeared on Formula One Ferraris. Fiat's awareness of the changing market place was also coming to the fore.

In the early days only enthusiasts bought Ferraris. By their very nature, these enthusiasts gratefully accepted what they were given. If a car had a very heavy clutch, or poor ventilation, well then that was the price that had to be paid. But as everyday cars got better, both in their handling and in their features, the demands on the super car manufacturers were growing all the time. Fiat, as makers of everyday cars, were, of course, aware of this.

But despite this awareness, they seemed to leave Ferrari to his own devices, so that when Testarossa's immediate predecessor, the Berlinetta Boxer arrived, it was in many ways still an enthusiasts-only car. With a body by Pininfarina, the 365 GT4BB was produced from 1971-1976. The term Boxer referred to its horizontally opposed piston arrangement which looked like two boxers fighting.

The Berlinetta Boxer changed shape in 1976, to become the 512. Pininfarina was again responsible for the change of clothes.

All the time emission regulations were getting tougher. In 1987, an 'i' appeared after the 512. Gone were the Weber triple choke carburettors, and in came the Bosch K-Jetronic indirect injection. Twenty horse power disappeared with the carburettors.

In America, federal regulations required impact absorbing bumpers – something that would have ruined the lines of the Berlinetta Boxer, so Enzo Ferrari simply refused to export to the States. Some cars made it over, but they were private imports. The beautiful BB was saved, but at a considerable price!

Behind the scenes, Fiat were balancing the books. A new car was needed, and it would need to meet all the regulations on both sides of the Atlantic. Ferrari were to chase the lucrative US market and Fiat would decide how Sophistication was the name of the game. Nevertheless it is important to realise that a process of evolution was under way, not an act of new creation.

Airconditioning, leather seats, hi-fi, lead-free petrol, even a muted exhaust note, were all part of what Squazzini (then managing director) called 'the 300

Ferrari drivers have won the World Championship nine times and the company has won the Constructors Championship eight times since 1958. Success on the race track has made the Ferrari the sports car of the stars

Enzo Ferrari was furious when Carlo Chiti, his chief engineer, set to work on a rear-engined experimental car in the late 1950s. Ferrari took a lot of persuading, but the Testarossa, and the fact that rear-engined cars have dominated Formula One ever since, vindicated his change of heart

Red hot and a cool green. Fiat's involvement in the development and design of the Testarossa for the American market ensured the use of lead-free petrol, making this the most environmentally-friendly Ferrari to date

kilometre per hour living room' when the Testarossa was launched at the Lido in the Champs Elysees on 2 October 1984. The leading journalists in Europe were wined and dined, and amid what can only be described as a party atmosphere, the Testarossa rose from beneath the floor! Red headed girls wearing thigh-length boots and bizarre head gear posed for photographers in front of the most prestigious cars ever built.

Next day, the Paris salon opened at the exhibition park at the Porte de Versailles. Fiat had judged it right – 37 orders were taken at the Paris show. Delivery dates were extended to two years. By the end of 1984 more than 110 cars had left Maranello.

In real terms, Testarossa has a short pedigree, back to 1947. But what a pedigree. In that (relatively) short time Ferraris have won eight Mille Miglias, nine wins in the Targa Florio, nine wins at Le Mans, nine Formula One drivers championships (representing over 90 Formula One victories) and 14 world titles for makes – a total of over 5,000 race victories.

But there's more to a real Ferrari, and make no mistake, this red head is a real Ferrari. There are those years when Enzo Ferrari raced cars himself, worked with Alfa Rome, and made them champions. Despite the comfort, into Testarossa go all those years of tears, determination and victory. In short, it has a soul.

At 15 mpg, the Testarossa's 25.3 gallon fuel tanks offer a useful range of just under 350 miles

The Engine – Soul of the Car

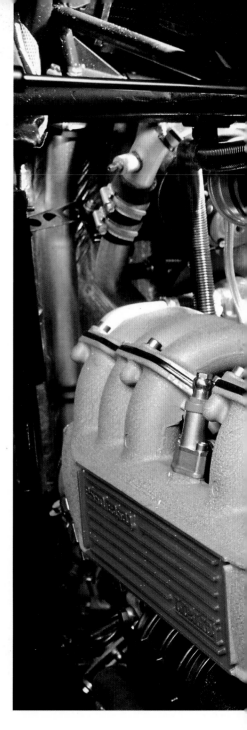

When describing the attributes of a Ferrari, it is not unusual to borrow from the language of music. Motor magazine for example (in its issue 13 July 1985) describes the engine sound as 'a muted growl of extraordinary purity'. Once, Ferrari had a letter from some young Americans telling him that, in their opinion, the music made by the engines of his cars was like that of the great symphonic composers. In her sensitive biography of Beethoven, Marion Scott sums up his violin concerto thus: 'Here is enshrined the soul of the Stradivarius violin'.

Interestingly Ferrari has himself been likened to that famous maker of stringed instruments. In 1960 Gianna Brera wrote 'And who pray is the greatest Italian today. I for my part am quite certain: Enzo Ferrari, the Stradivari of the motor racing world'.

The Stradivari of the motor racing world for his part was in no doubt that 'engines have a soul'. Furthermore, he asserted that 'engines are like sons: one settles down and studies and another signs cheques and is dissolute'. If any doubt remains about how central to a Ferrari is the engine, consider what Ferrari himself said; 'I build engines, and attach wheels to them'.

Soon after the war, Ferrari revived his passion for the racing car. Providentially, Gioacchino Colomba showed up at Marenello, looking for a fresh start. The genius of Alfa Romeo's 158 put his skills at Ferrari's disposal.

They worked at a shared dream – to build a 12 cylinder engine. Ferrari himself had nurtured this dream since 1914, when he saw photographs of an Indianopolis-racing 12 cylinder Packard. Their dream became a reality, resulting in a V12 with a capacity of 1497 cc, in 1947. The cylinder banks were inclined at 60 degrees and the cylinders themselves had a bore and stroke of 55.0 x 52.5 mm. Increasing the bore and stroke to 59.0 x 58.8 mm resulted in a larger 1902 cc engine suitable for the newly planned Formula Two racing category. This saw the start of a numeric system for numbering the engines based on the cubic capacity (in cms) of one cylinder. The bore diameter was steadily increased, while the stroke remained constant.

Aurelio Lampredi replaced Colombo in 1949 and designed the engine known as the 'long block' (due to an increase in length of 102 mm). This engine, designed with the 4.5 litre unsupercharged Formula One limit in mind, used many of the features inherent in Colombo's design, but with greater centre bore spacings (of 108 mm) thus allowing an increase in overall cubic capacities. Development continued on both engines, which were produced in a variety of sizes for many years.

1956 was the year in which the first 'large volume' unit was produced, the 250. Production rose steadily to the present, although during the first 10 years, the average seems to have been around one car a week.

Ferrari continued to attract the gifted engineers. Mauro Forghieri took the road to Maranello in 1960 and like his predecessor Colombo, set about designing

Enzo Ferrari himself said that 'engines have a soul'. If proof were needed as to how important the engine is to a Ferrari, consider his statement that 'I build engines and attach wheels to them'

When the Testarossa greeted the press
at the Paris Lido, the red finish to the
cylinder heads denoted more than a colour
addition to the F102. The Testarossa's
engine (known as F113A) was reminiscent
of pre-turbo Formula One engines

a 12 cylinder engine. In 1963 Ferrari announced the debut of two new engines, designed for Grand Prix racing. One was a V8, and it went on to power John Surtees to a Formula One world championship in the following year. The other engine was Forghieri's 12 cylinder – not a V12 but a flat 12. This engine of 1500 cc was used in the same chassis as the V8 and was known as 1512FI, and also as 512FI. It was run alongside the V8 in late 1964 and throughout the 1965 season.

The flat 12 grew by 500 cc to 2 litres, and powered Peter Schetty to a magnificent European Mountain Championship in the 212E Montagna, in 1969. By the time Forghieri had been at Maranello 10 years, he had developed the flat 12 engine to 3 litres and this engine powered a sports racer, the 312PB which was run experimentally for the 1971 season, and in earnest during the new 3 litre series in 1972. The car swept the board, achieving victory in all ten rounds of the championship.

Forghieri also designed a new Formula One car for this magnificent engine. This car, known as 312B, was a disappointment, requiring considerable chassis and suspension development. Forghieri persevered, however, and by 1975 his cars had carried Nikki Lauda to the world championship. Two years later, Lauda repeated this triumph and the flat 12s took Jody Scheckter to his world title in 1979.

By then, of course, the boxer had been working happily in the 365 GT4/BB, its cubic capacity enlarged to 4.4 litres. At the heart of this engine was one of Ferrari's masterpieces. The crankshaft was machined from a solid piece of chrome molybdenum steel. Forged connecting rods paired off on the six throws and the crankshaft turned in seven main bearings. The light alloy pistons moved in cast iron liners which had a bore centre dimension of 95 mm, and the block itself was forged of silomin at the Maranello foundry. Each light alloy head contained two camshaft which activated the valves directly.

For the first time on a Ferrari engine (also appearing on the 308 GT4, 8 cylinder at the same time) toothed belts replaced the camshaft driving chains. Lubrication was by wet sump, and each cylinder bank has its own oil filter. The gear box was placed not at the rear of the engine, as it had been on the prototypes, but under the engine. Horse power was quoted at 360-380 at 7700 rpm. Maximum torque, occurred at 3900 rpm of 303 ft/lbs (42mkg).

The changes to five litres for the 512BB in 1976 resulted from the bore dimension being increased from 81 mm to 82 mm and the stroke lengthened from 71 to 78 mm, due to the use of a new crankshaft. Dry sump lubrication was adopted, and although the compression was higher at 9.2:1, horse power remained the same, but at 6800 rpm, 900 rpm less than before. The major improvement was in the area of torque, which was 10 per cent greater. In its fuel injected version this engine was known as F102.

When Testarossa greeted the European press at the Paris Lido, the red crackle finish on its cylinder heads denoted more than a colour addition to F102. Testarossa's engine (known as F113A) was more reminiscent of the pre-turbo Formula One engines. Compared to F102, F113A was 20 kilograms lighter, had 50 hp more (390 hp at 6300 rpm) and four kgm more torque (50 mkg at 4500 rpm). The quest for more power meant considering the application of a turbocharger, but this was considered inappropriate for the Ferrari flagship (despite the 208 model in 1983). The solution settled on was that of four valves per cylinder, an arrangement which allowed exhaust and inlet valve overlap to be reduced, a happy arrangement since fuel injection has the notorious habit of squirting some neat fuel out through the exhaust when both valves remain open, in a most environmentally unfriendly way!

To further increase efficiency and reduce pollution still further, the mechanical Bosch K-Jetronic fuel injection was scrapped in favour of the same makers KE-Jetronic system, full of sophisticated electronics.

As with F102, the cylinder block and heads are forged from a silicon and aluminium alloy known as silumin, favoured for its strength and light weight, but instead of the shrunk-in cast iron cylinder liners, F113A uses aluminium liners, coated with Nickasil (to reduce bore wear). The 12 pistons are not made at Maranello, but bought in from Mahle. The crankshaft, made of forged molybdenum steel is made outside, and bought in, to be machined in the Maranello foundry and the bearing surfaces are nitrided. The exhaust valves are made of nimonic steel, while plain steel suffices for the inlet valves, which are inclined (two per cylinder) at an angle of 20 degrees. The exhaust valves are set at an angle of 21 degrees. The seats are cast iron; the guides are made of bronze.

The engine features twin overhead cams for each bank of cylinders. The valve timing control is belt driven, using cogged tooth belts of the Goodyear Supertorque PD type, which are able to absorb the thermal expansion of the engine, without becoming stressed in the process. The tensioner is adjusted semi-automatically.

Each bank of cylinders gets its own distributor, and also its own coil to pass electricity to the spark plugs. Each plug has a stem tread of 12 mm diameter, as on the Ferraro GTO, in order to sit in the best position in the combustion chamber.

Dry sump lubrication is provided by two scavenger pumps and one pressure pump, working via an oil reservoir and a thermostatically controlled radiator.

Strictly speaking, Forghieri's engine is not a 'true' boxer, in that the engines of the Porsche 911, VW Beetle, Citroen 2CV and GS, (all air cooled) or the water cooled Lancia Gamma or Alfa Sud, have opposite pistons working in different directions. Because the connecting rods are paired, the directly opposing pistons travel in the same direction in the Ferrari engine, a tried and tested configuration used on the V12 engine, in the quest to reduce secondary imbalance stresses.

Siting a 12 cylinder engine behind the driver leaves little room for anything else. The advantage of the Boxer configuration is the low overall height of the engine enabling the gear box and differential to be situated underneath in a single cast piece of silumin (but of course the engine and gear box are separately lubricated). Even with this arrangement, the engine is effectively the same height as the driver's shoulders!

The overall compactness of the engine, gearbox and differential assembly means that the engine sits high in the car. Compare the height here with the head restraints visible through the rear window. This high centre of gravity can cause twitchiness above 150 mph

The decision to mount the radiators (water and oil) at the side of the car (here the oil radiator is clearly visible) meant that the Testarossa could have a proper boot

In the Berlinetta boxer, a particularly neat installation was achieved, but with one important compromise. In order to limit the overall length of the car, the radiator was sited at the front (the normal method of circumventing this problem, on four or eight cylinder models is to mount them transversely, as in the Dino, or Mira, but with a big, square engine, there really is no gain in a 90 degree turn).

With a low, sleek bonnet, a radiator and spare wheel leave little space for luggage, and the Berlinetta's touring ability was seriously impaired. Furthermore, the pipes connecting the radiator to the engine ran through the passenger compartment, making long summer journeys a touch on the warm side!

When Pininfarina was given the task of designing Testarossa, the first styling exercise showed a very strong BB influence, featuring a large rear glass area, following the falling roof line to the tail, curving down to the tops of the wheel arches. The radiator was still at the front however, and then, quite suddenly, Ferrari decided to mount it amidships. Of all the decisions taken, this one would have the most impact on the shape the car would take.

Sergio Pininfarina, whose studio was responsible for the design of Testarossa, said that 'this characteristic, more than any other, influenced the shape of the car and its personality'.

Once Ferrari had the radiator position cast in stone, Pininfarina soon arrived at that most distinctive element of the Testarossa's design

Design and assembly

With the decision made as to where to site the coolers, Pininfarina could start work again. The next set of designs, perhaps surprisingly, still do not feature that most characteristic feature of the car – the huge elongated slats that start a few inches behind the door hinge line and extend to about eight inches in front of the back wheels. The huge, swept-up line of the rear wing did feature, however, providing vast aerodynamic aid, and allowing for a much bigger increase in rear track compared to the Berlinetta Boxer (A number of people incidentally, felt that the BB was undertyred, a situation that Testarossa's body style would easily remedy).

Already it was certain that the car would be wedge shaped. After all, putting in a mid-mounted engine with mid-mounted radiators, wide rear tyres and a shape that allowed stability at speeds up to 180 miles per hour does rather limit the shape!

What is remarkable is the extent to which Pininfarina was able to work the shape into one of the most distinctive and instantly recognisable cars around, and, in the next set of designs the Testarossa of today is clearly recognisable – the main difference being whether to keep the sloping back window or opt for an upright rear glass and flat engine cover. Weight savings, ease of manufacture, and more efficient engine cooling were the reasons given for finally deciding on the latter solution.

The first designs date from 1978, but it was not until the end of 1981 that a shape emerged that was considered suitable for wind tunnel testing. Once Ferrari had approved the design, Pininfarina set about making a full scale model first in polystyrene and after some development, a model for wind testing was built in resin. To this model short strands of wool were attached at intervals all over the body, and their interaction with air flow was measured.

In this way, the flow of air required for engine cooling could be observed and the side apertures were gradually enlarged and shaped to maximise efficiency. The design had the car at full width already, and making the car even wider to enlarge the apertures was not really an option. Regulations decreed that entry into such an orifice must be prevented, either by mesh, or a form of grille, and so the famous long slats came into being. Not only do they prevent the ingress of curious hands (when stationery), or passing rabbits (when on the move), but they absolutely maximise the huge flow of air necessary to cool the engine, without in any way upsetting the handling properties of the car. The growth of the slab like rear wings from behind the front wheel arch was also for a purpose – to generate negative lift, and minimal drift – facts that cannot be too highly stressed when looking at speeds above 150 mph.

In fact the Cz factor was nil on the rear axle and only slightly positive at the front axle.

The first designs date from 1978, but it was not until the end of 1981 that a shape emerged that was considered suitable for wind tunnel testing. The first full-scale model was made from polystyrene

In side elevation, the shape of the roof can be seen as tear-shaped, an idea that Citroen was working on in 1955 with the Ds, and later on GS and CX, as a means to aid the flow of air quickly over the car to a squared-off tail, where it broke away cleanly, with a minimum of power-sucking turbulence.

Flying buttresses, made familiar by Jaguar on the XJS, continue the tear-drop beautifully, without encroaching too much on rearward vision. The Dino, of course, also used flying buttresses, but the laurels for first use of this device on a Ferrari go to another Pininfarina design, the wonderful 375 Mille Miglia Berlinetta of 1954. This car, built for Ingrid Bergman (who never took delivery) also incorporated retractable headlights, and a dynamic air intake for the carburettors.

On the Testarossa, the top section of the buttresses is finished in satin black, and incorporates an effective outlet for air from the passenger compartment.

The engine compartment lid and buttresses are hinged above the rear window, at the back of the roof line. The lid itself is comprised of 34 horizontal black slats, which form a huge grille pointing skywards. In order to minimize intrusion of the elements, and to effect a small degree of sound deadening, a square painted panel covers almost half of the grille, from the rear window, back to the last ten slats. Stylistically it works most effectively.

The engine cover has a raised lip at its rearmost edge to improve airflow, but this is most discreet – nothing so vulgar as a spoiler! The rear bumper is a neat, wrap around affair, which carries the number plate, and above which sits the rear lights, and indicators. These lights are covered by a black full width grid, whose purpose is to prevent a build up of dirt caused by road spray, and is a Pininfarina patent.

At the front of the roof is the huge flush fitting windscreen which is bonded to the steel pillars and roof. Set at an angle, the glass sweeps down to the low front, which gently curves to the oddly blunt nose.

The front bumper incorporates a grille. Not of course to cool the radiator, but to direct air to the front brakes. Fog lights, indicators and parking lights are all set into the bumper. The headlights are covered and are retractable, the frontal angle being too great to house anything but 'pop up' lights. Under the bumper is a chin spoiler, discreet in black, and featuring a little duct on the car's left, which provides air to the airconditioning condenser. The bonnet lifts up to reveal a genuinely usable boot of approximately 3.5 cubic feet. Underneath the boot floor sits a 'space saver' spare wheel equipped with a 115/85 R18 tyre. At the front is a container for the windscreen washer reservoir.

The bonnet is made from aluminium, and is rolled by hand, as are all the other panels, including the roof and doors, which are made from steel coated with zinc, chrome and then with chrome oxide. This anti-corrosive process was developed by Ferrari, and is called Zincro X. The chassis and body are not made by Ferrari, but by a small specialist company called ITCA, who are based 150 miles from Maranello. The chassis is made, not in the form of a monocoque, but rather from tubing in the old fashioned way of the artisan. As far as rigidity is concerned, Ferrari claims an improvement over the monocoque, but the chief advantage of a sectionalised chassis is the ease with which changes to type approval can be accommodated. With a monocoque, it would take a year to introduce a modification, whereas as things stand, a change can be incorporated in production within a month.

The tubular frame has a detachable rear section to facilitate removal of the power plant. Completed bodies and chassis are taken from ITCA to nearby Grugliasco, where Pininfarina's factory is situated. On arrival, the bodies are degreased, rinsed and then immersed in zinc phosphate. After drying in a huge oven, body and chassis are primed in an electrically charged dip. After curing, two more coats of primer are applied. Mastic sealer is then applied to all inner panel seams and joints, followed by undersealing. Even now, the body is not yet ready for painting. In what is an extraordinary exercise in hand finishing, the bodies are rubbed down by skilled craftsmen and then given another coat of primer. Next comes another electrically charged coat, but this time in the customer's choice of colour. All accessible areas of the shell are painted in this way; remaining areas are hand sprayed. The interior is painted matt black, and a final lacquer is applied to the exterior before final finishing via an oven.

The car now moves down a production line where the glass is glued into place with a spin off from the space programme – a self sealing flexible mastic which soon hardens to make a glass to metal bond which adds considerably to the overall body stiffness.

The wiring loom is fitted, followed by body trim, electrical parts, sound absorbing materials and panels, airconditioning, sealing rubbers, steering column, instruments bumpers, the headlamps and their operating motors.

Finally the seats are fitted, and the cars are then sent to Maranello for the installation of brakes, engines and ancillaries. Here the engine/transmission/rear suspension unit will have already been attached to the detachable sub–chassis, and now the whole assembly is offered up to the main chassis, from below. At the front, the steering racks, and front suspension are installed. At the same time, the exhaust is fitted, followed by the wheels.

Essential fluids are checked, and the car is then road tested, and returned for adjustments, both mechanical and cosmetic. The total man hours amounts to around 500.

As previously mentioned, the foundry at Maranello has no facilities for casting steel, but the engine, transmission and suspension castings are all produced in-house. Moulds are coated with sand from France, or earth from Sarona, a process which eases the cast item's removal. Carbonic gas and bonding agents are injected into the matrix, which is then baked, the whole process being designed to harden the matrix, which is then heated with a blow gun to purge it of harmful gases. A number of moulds may be joined at this point, to make a final larger matrix.

Into this mould molten alloy is poured, after being heated to a temperature of 600 degrees celsius in Maranello's underground furnaces. Large quantities of silumin and magnesium are melted and from the mass a small amount is taken for

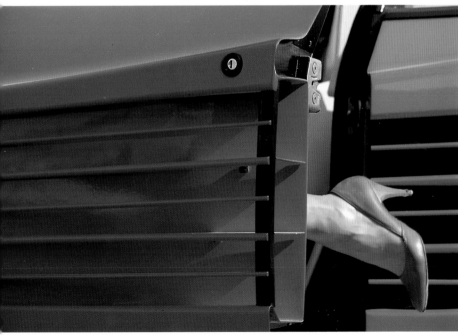

The elongated slats dominate the design. Starting a few inches behind the door hinge line, they extend to eight inches in front of the back wheel

Although ugly to some, the slats are an integral part of the Testarossa's performance. During wind tunnel testing, Pininfarina attached strands of wool to the sides to measure their interaction with air flow. In this way, the flow of air required for engine cooling could be observed

chemical analysis in the adjacent laboratory. Assuming satisfactory tests,
the molten metal will be cast. To give some idea of the size of the operation each
engine block takes 50 kg of silumin, and 10 blocks will be cast at the same time!

The entire operation is monitored by a computer, which keeps a watchful eye
on temperature fluctuations. It is vital that the moulds cool at a steady rate,
any rapid change in temperature will cause the metal to 'stress', producing invisible
brittle zones. Once hardened, the moulds are gently heated for six minutes,
then applied vibration frees the moulding from the matrix. Some numbering,
symbols etc. will be inherent in the mould, and others such as the date,
and employee identification code will be stamped on using a die punch.

The use of partial automation of the engine assembly has seen the workforce
in this area reduce by two-thirds (although it has actually grown in other areas)
and although this is a highly skilled and labour intensive operation it is possible to
produce as many as 70 Boxer blocks in one day.

'Casting machining' is an area where drilling, tapping and finishing are carried
out automatically, using Mandelli machines controlled by a Digital VAXII/750
computer. The savings in man hours can only be guessed at, but there are some
things better done by machine, and Ferrari (Fiat) very wisely installed equipment
to do these things: outrun, or 'flash' is knocked off with a hammer, and the cast
item is then finished of with power tools before being polished. Various tests to
check the quality of the casting are then performed. Samples from a batch are
subjected to further tests. In the laboratory, the casting is visually enlarged 1500
times, to check for minute cracks, stress points, or any visible defect, however
small. This is followed by x-raying and analysis with a spectrometer and a 1500
volt spectroscope. The use of fully automatic robots was introduced by Fiat, but
on an extremely gradual basis, over the years. Known as the Flexible
Manufacturing System, the idea uses robots for those boring and repetitive
machining operations, leaving the skilled work to artisans, who assemble the
magnificent engines, starting with the crankcase to which are fitted the elements
needed to make the engine live; its heart in the shape of the molybdenum
crankshaft, with bearings and cylinder liners followed by pistons, con rods and
big end bearings. Then come the cylinder heads – those Testarossi. When the
fuel injection and electrical systems are added, the engine is mated to the
previously assembled transmission unit, and is then taken to a sound proofed
room where each and every engine is run for a minimum of four hours. The
entire engine manufacture, from casting to test bed takes 18 working days!

During design, the apertures were gradually enlarged to maximise the huge flow of air necessary to cool the engine without upsetting the handling properties of the car

Above the grille is the huge aerodynamic
sweep that becomes the rear wing.
The growth of the wings from behind the
front wheel arch was to generate
negative lift and minimal drift

Seen from this angle the immense proportions of that upswept area are clear. The resulting C_z factor is nil on the rear axle and only slightly positive at the front axle – a fact that cannot be too highly stressed when travelling at speeds over 150 mph

Above

In side elevation the shape of the roof can be seen as teardrop. This aids the flow of air quickly over the car to a squared off tail where it breaks away cleanly, with a minimum of power sucking turbulence. The flying buttresses continue the tear-drop perfectly, without spoiling too much rear vision

Left

The engine compartment lid and buttresses are hinged at the roof line for engine access. The lid itself comprises 34 slats which form a huge grille pointing skywards

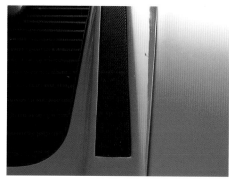

Above
The gentle drop of the flying buttresses incorporates extractors – effective outlets for stale air from the passenger compartment. The top section of the buttresses is finished in satin black

Left
The rear lights are covered by a black, full-width grid, the purpose of which is to prevent a build-up of dirt caused by road spray. This is a Pininfarina patent

The Car

There are very few bad cars produced these days. In areas of safety, vast improvements have taken place. On the Testarossa, servo assistance is courtesy of Bendatalia in the form of a brake booster, which operates a relief valve to prevent rear wheel lock up should a heavy-footed driver stamp on the middle pedal! Few road tests reveal anything other than good brakes for example.

True, one reviewer may prefer the 'feel' of the brakes on brand X, another may find them spongy, or lacking in 'bite' but these are peripheral values; that the car will stop when asked is taken for granted. Furthermore the availability of anti-lock systems means less skill is required from the driver in adverse conditions.

Enzo Ferrari was, it seems, not a man to give praise easily. When Lancia handed over all its racing equipment in 1955 and Fiat guaranteed that five-year donation, Ferrari stayed at Modena, missing the ceremony at Turin. To have been present would have necessitated a public admission of thanks!

But throughout his working life Enzo Ferrari held one man with unwavering high esteem; Tazio Nuvolari, described by Ferrari as 'the one truly great racing driver'. He went on to say 'there is always a perfect balance between a car and its driver – 50 per cent car and 50 per cent driver'. With Nuvolari, this relationship was completely overturned: he contributed at least 75 per cent of the total'.

When Ferrari built road cars, he was probably aware of the comparative lack of skill that some of the owners possessed. After all, a large wallet buys the car, not the ability to drive it! With Fiat on board, knowing the high competence of the family car, a lot of money would have to go into making Testarossa a more failsafe car. Perhaps the relationship of car to driver is now 75 per cent to 25 per cent – this time in favour of the car!

Certainly the brakes are massive: 12.16 in (30.9 cm) ventilated discs at the front, 12.20 in (31.0 cm) with four pot callipers at the rear. The cable-operated handbrake works on miniature rear drums. Incidentally, there is a curiously British influence on the adoption of disc brakes by Ferrari. In the year that he became world champion, Mike Hawthorn was unhappy with the brakes on his Ferrari. Enzo Ferrari was adamant that drum brakes were sufficient, but by the time of the Italian Grand Prix, Hawthorn had had his way and his car was fitted out with disc brakes.

At the end of the season, Hawthorn retired from Formula One racing, and the Ferrari team, taking as a memento the car that won him the championship. For the following year, all the Ferrari team cars sported disc brakes. Sadly, in January 1959, Hawthorn was killed at the wheel of a Jaguar in an accident that seems to have been an unfortunate mixture of rain and high speed, and a 'race' with a friend's Mercedes.

But back to Testarossa where the rear biased weight distribution (approximately 41 per cent front to 59 per cent rear) becomes obvious when you consider that the rack and pinion steering is non-assisted.

Independent suspension is fitted front and rear by double wishbone with a single Koni damper unit at the front. Mounted in rubber bushes, the lower wishbones are of the wide-based variety and are cross-braced for additional tension

*Rear suspension differs in using not one,
but two coil spring damper units per
wheel. One is set adjacent to the
wishbones. The lower wishbone is
attached to an anti-roll bar, as up front*

There is a choice of footwear, from Goodyear or Michelin. At the front Eagle 225/50 NR16 or TRX (MXX) 240/45 VR415 and at the rear, Eagle 255/50 VR16 or TRX (MXX) 280/45 VR415. That these huge areas of rubber can be accommodated says something of the width of the car compared to the Berlinetta Boxer, from 183 to 198 cms! This increase in width was not, incidentally, merely to incorporate the radiator and oil cooler (an increase in wheelbase by five cms aided this, but to incorporate the fantastic aerodynamic advantages offered by that sweeping shell that becomes the rear wing.

The radiator sits on the car's left hand side when fitted. Laterally opposite sits the oil radiator – a fan assisted heat exchanger to cool the 27 pints (15.5 litres) of oil that are this engine's life blood. On the Berlinetta Boxer these positions were occupied by two fuel tanks. Testarossa's single fuel tank sits between the engine and the passenger compartment, safely tucked away from rupturing impacts. The capacity is 115 litres of unleaded petrol, with a further 18 litres in a reserve tank. Compared with the Berlinetta Boxer, the diameter of the double-disk clutch is increased from 8.5 in to 9.5 in, in order to cope with the increase in both power and torque.

The gearbox is Ferrari's own, a five speed box (plus reverse) with final drive via a ZF limited slip differential, with hypoid bevel gears (the final drive ratio is 3.21:1 (14/45).

To keep this big car on the road and to save its occupants from unnecessary jars and jolts, independent suspension is fitted front and rear. At the front, tubular steel derived double wishbones are used, naturally with anti-dive geometry. Lower wishbones are of the wide-based variety and are cross-braced for additional tension. They are mounted in rubber bushes. The combined spring-damper unit sits between each pair of wishbones, and the uprights are of cast alloy, made at the foundry. To the lower wishbone on each side is attached an anti-roll bar.

The rear suspension differs in using not one, but two coil spring damper units per side; one is set adjacent to the (again cross-braced) wishbones. On the rear lower wishbone is attached one anti-roll bar, as up front. The turning circle (arrived after 3.5 turns lock to lock) is just over 39 ft.

The massive ventilated disc brakes: 30.9 cm at the front and 31.0 cm, with four pot callipers, at the rear. Ferrari's use of disc brakes goes back to the Italian Grand Prix of 1958, when Mike Hawthorn refused to race with drum brakes

The rear suspension, clearly showing the
lower wishbone driveshaft and the anti-
roll bar. The combined spring-damper
unit sits between each pair of wishbones
and the uprights are of cast alloy

Above
*The cabin is trimmed in leather,
with Connolly leather on the seats –
cream in the case of the right-hand
drive example*

Right
*Black leather is used for the seats in this
left-hand drive Testarossa. Airconditioning
means that darker colours can be used
with no fear of cabin heat build up*

The hand brake is beautifully sited. It is cable operated and works on miniature rear drums

The gear selector is a joy to use.
The gearbox is a Ferrari design of five
speeds (plus reverse), with final drive
via a ZF limited slip differential with
hypoid bevel gears. The final drive ratio is
3.21:1 (14/45)

*Fog lights (front and rear), heated rear
screen and map reading lights are all
situated above your head*

The Testarossa's rear biased weight distribution (approximately 41 per cent front/59 per cent rear) becomes obvious when you consider that the front and pinion steering is non-assisted

Heating and other minor controls are set in between the occupants' seats. The instrumentation looks cheap, as does the Ferrari devised switchgear. The radio hides away when not in use

Straps to retain Ferrari's own leather luggage are fitted behind the seats; a vital touring aid when you consider that this car has a boot space of 3.5 cubic feet above the space saving spare wheel and the 115/85 R18 tyre

*At the front of the car are the air horns
and the windscreen washer reservoir*

The grille at the top of the boot is sited for a large throughput of air when the car is on the move. The duct in the spoiler under the right headlamp is for the supply of cooling air for the airconditioning condenser

Left
The Dino also used flying buttresses, but the laurels for the first use of this device on a Ferrari go to another Pininfarina design, the wonderful 375 Mille Miglia Berlinetta of 1954

Below
The bonnet is made from aluminium and is rolled by hand, but as with the Berlinetta Boxer, the Testarossa's body and chassis are not made by Ferrari. Whereas the Boxer was bodied by Scaglietti in Modena, the Testarossa is bodied 150 miles away by a small specialist company called ITCA

The engine cover has a raised lip at its rearmost edge to improve airflow. Nothing so vulgar as a spoiler. Note the neat, wrap-around bumper

A car with a lot of appeal, but well beyond the means of most wallets. Few Testarossa owners do more than 20,000 miles a year. Most cars only do between 4000 and 6000 miles a year. A new Testarossa will cost you in excess of £120,000, but you could pick up a high-mileage car for around £85,000

What is in no doubt is the sheer stylishness of Pininfarina's design. This car is every inch a star

Above
*The front bumper incorporates a grille;
not of course to cool the radiator, but to
direct air to the front brakes*

Opposite
*The headlights are covered and retractable,
the front angle being too great to house
anything but pop up lights*

Overleaf
*With the headlights down there is no
visible front end from the driving seat.
The pop-up lights give a useful reference
in tight situations such as car parks.*

The rear mirror gave a superb view over that immense rear wing, but obstructed a huge chunk of three quarters of front vision, making junctions a nightmare

Left
There were few negative reactions when the car was launched, but much criticism was levelled at the siting of the exterior rear-view mirror. At first, only one was fitted, midway down the windscreen pillar. The front bumper incorporates the fog lamps and indicators

Moving the mirror to a lower position on the door overcame the front view problem with only a marginal rear view compromise

The Testarossa complements any environment be it a crowded inner city street, or the lush green fields of a country landscape

As well as moving the mirror down it was decided to fit them in pairs in an attempt to gain as much visibility over the vast rear end as possible. Designed by Pininfarina and manufactured by Gilardini, the mirror has been described as a periscope and, along with the side vents, epitomise the Testarossa's style

Around Modena

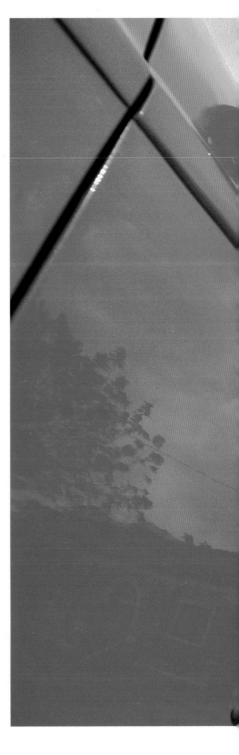

Maranello sits in the foot hills of the Apennines, just 17 kilometres from Modena. When Enzo Ferrari moved from the Scuderia to the foot of the so called 'Gothic Line' in 1943 it was because he owned a piece of land in the immediate vicinity of the site of the now famous present factory, in the heartland of a naturally plenteous fertile region. Less than 50 kms away is Parma, famous for the ham that takes its name, and the local cheese, Parmesan. The local wine of Modena is Lambrusco, a light sparkling wine in red and white, and drunk in copious quantities locally, in a very light red form, almost a rose.

Pasta, sausages, cheeses, preserves, and textiles are all around you in Modena. Here people eat well, drink well and live life to the full.

You might think that Ferraris were two a penny here, after all they are tested on the local roads as well as the Fiorano track. But arrival at local towns for a photogaphy session brought crowds round the car, and stopped traffic! Such is the passion for life. A similar exercise in Windsor produced no interest at all (this could have been a Ford Escort!). But the English are a reserved people, not given to waving at cars, even if a prancing horse sits on its yellow badge!

In the foothills of the Appenines, every village has people who will wave at your passing, who smile as the red car winds on up towards Mount Cimone. On these winding roads you realise what a triumph Ferrari has achieved with this car. The amazing torque means that the constant gear-changing that is mandatory with an Alfa-Romeo, is largely unnecessary. Going down a cog gets the dust flying, and makes passing a local in a primitive delivery van nothing less than a mild flick of the wrist and ankle.

Even in Germany there are few places where 180 mph is feasible, at least on a day to day basis, and for the rest of Europe, or America there is nowhere short of a race track. Plenty of cars will reach 150 mph and quite a few of them will do so safely, with braking to match. But few cars will top the 170, let alone 180 mph of Testarossa. The experience really gets the adrenalin pumping. At 150 mph Testarossa sits well on the road. Add more right foot and you become aware of just how high that engine sits behind you. The aerodynamics are beautiful, but the high centre of gravity causes post 150 mph twitches and constant correction is needed through the steering wheel. But 180 mph is attainable and is there on tap. What really impresses is the acceleration, 60 mph arrives in five seconds. In this car, overtaking involves constant brainwork, in judging distances and other vehicle's speeds, but it is always a pleasure, since the car is over responsive, eager to act, swift to carry out your will. Only a fool need get into difficulties on a public road. Not all questions are sensible questions; 'what shape is yellow?' is as sensible as asking Testarossa to fly over a hump back bridge at three figures. Don't laugh, it happened, and took the roof off the car coming the other way, and its occupants' heads in the process.

Just as the Modena architecture, this is true Italian style

Even if this car is built, as I believe, with an expectation of 25 per cent driver 75 per cent car, that still leaves 25 per cent of extreme variability. For his sports cars, Ferrari was proudest of the fact that the entity was so well rounded. Around that jewel of an engine he did not in fact merely 'attach wheels'. There is a lovely story, told by Ferrari himself, about Ferrucio Lamborghini, who had a passion for supercars (before he built his own). Lamborghini would apparently get hold of a sports car and head for the motorway, where he would accelerate to 200kph and slip into neutral. Then he would count the number of kilometres he could coast!

'Mine ran the furthest' said Ferrari, 'very nice of him'!

Given a good understanding driver this car makes music, from the jazz syncopations of rubber to the regular thump, thump of concrete sectioned motorways, recalling bygone days of steam, before tracks were welded. But this is music of the road, picked up in passing. For music of the soul cast an ear behind you, where twelve cylinders remind you that the musical heritage is Rossini and Verdi!

Left and following pages
Once assembled the cars are test driven around the towns and countryside of Maranello and Modena, wearing the special 'Prova' licence plates. They are then returned for adjustments, both mechanical and cosmetic. The total man hours involved in constructing a Testarossa amounts to around 500

*Modena is in the foothills of the Appenines,
an area providing spectacular views*

Right
At 150 mph, the Testarossa sits well on the road. Add more right foot and you become aware of just how high the engine sits behind you

Overleaf
The aerodynamics are beautiful, but the high centre of gravity causes post 150 mph twitches and constant correction is needed through the steering wheel

Right
With an acceleration of 0-60 mph in five seconds, overtaking in this car involves constant brainwork in judging distances and other vehicles' speeds. It is always a pleasure, however, as the car is so responsive

Overleaf
Given these surroundings, how many other cars can boast such beautiful test conditions

Speeding around these wonderful bends towards the town of Modena

Ferrari moved back from Milan to Modena
at the end of 1929. This is where he
founded the Scuderia. Enzo was fiercely
attached to his home town

Left, above and overleaf
The abundance of castles in this region emphasizes the countryside's fertility and the need to protect the area's wealth. It is fitting that the Testarossa does not look out of place in these surroundings. However, it must be remembered that the Testarossa was not 'graced' at Modena, but at Grugliasco by Pininfarina

A castle courtyard provides an opportunity to check items, but a parked Testarossa will always arouse interest . . . especially from someone who might remember the golden days of Nuvolari!

The great triumph of the Pininfarina design was the integration of all the aerodynamic devices into the shape of the car. Certainly a car to be seen with

This car has classic status. Park the Testarossa anywhere in Italy (or Britain, for that matter) and just watch the crowds gather

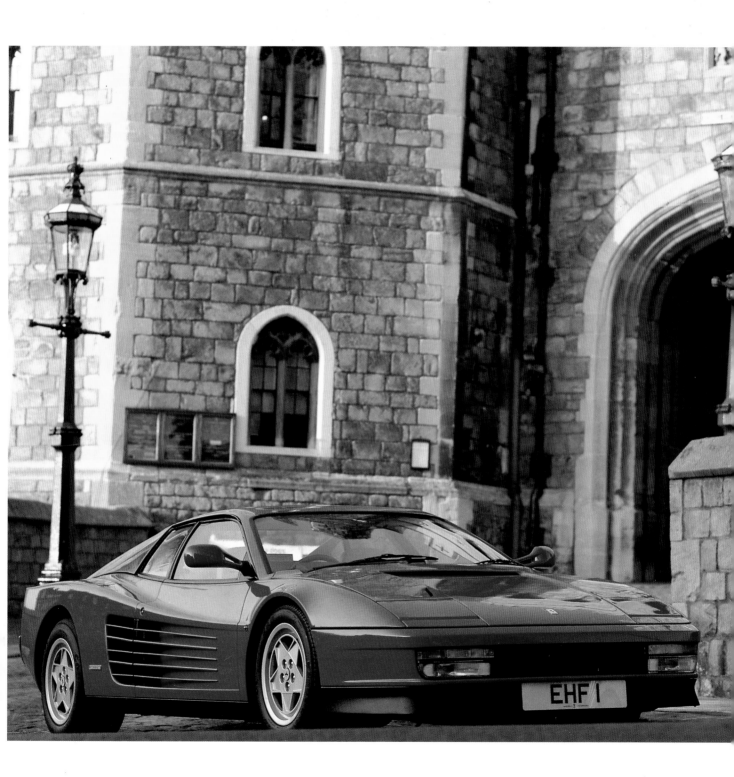

Shaken and stirred

'The M25 has been my best sales aid' says Mike Wilds with a smile. 'Traffic in London, particularly if you are trying to go from the west to the east, as a lot of my clients do, is dreadful.' Mike Wilds spends his days at a greenfield aerodrome to the west of London, selling helicopters.

If you are going to brave the M25, it has to be said that cruising the fast lane in a Ferrari Testarossa is a wonderful way to go. Wilds can see the attraction of the thick-set two seater: he was, for a short while, a Grand Prix driver and originally learned to fly when he raced on Sundays and idled throughout the week.

Comparing a Ferrari Testarossa to a Robinson R22 helicopter as pure business transportation is unfair, of course. You can use the £123,119.05 Ferrari as a commuter car: the smoothness and tractability of the massive five-litre flat-12 engine makes it a pussycat in traffic. But could you turn your back and leave the sleek aluminium panels to the tender mercies of the great unwashed, shopping trolleys akimbo, in a multi-storey car park?

And while the Robinson is as cute-as-a-button, it lacks decent luggage space and, like any helicopter, the swish-chop noise from the rotors grates and the bare-naked interior is far from luxurious. As business transportation, it has to be said, neither can offer the same mix of overall refinement, practicality, ease-of-use and thoughtful interior design that characterises the Vauxhall Cavalier. And you could buy a Cavalier with the amount the government bags as VAT on the Ferrari or the Robinson.

In theory, you could try and justify ownership of either of these invigorating machines by relishing the fact that each is perfectly content cruising at 100mph, and therefore offers a distinctive alternative to letting the train take the strain. Yet the seemingly omnipotent presence of those dark-suited gentlemen in a dayglo-striped Range Rover prevents you using the Ferrari's considerable performance day in, day out; similarly, should the cloud base fall too low, then the Robinson becomes a paperweight for the duration.

Helicopters, of course, are generally regarded as expensive ego-toys for the businessman who has everything: a Bell Jetranger will set you back around £380,000, for example. But the Robinson is as close as helicoptery has come to providing wings for the masses.

A Robinson R22 can be yours for £78,000 + VAT, subject to the dollar/sterling exchange rate not coming over too iffy. That's £45,000 – or a BMW 735 – cheaper than the Ferrari, if you can claim the VAT back, which is possible under certain circumstances. There are less costly Ferraris, too: the entry-level Mondialet props up the price list at £66,923.

Robinson, based in Torrance, California, is the opposite of Ferrari. The Italian manufacturer, now owned by Fiat, combines high-tech, hand-crafting, heritage and limited production to create iconic cars. There is said to be a three-year

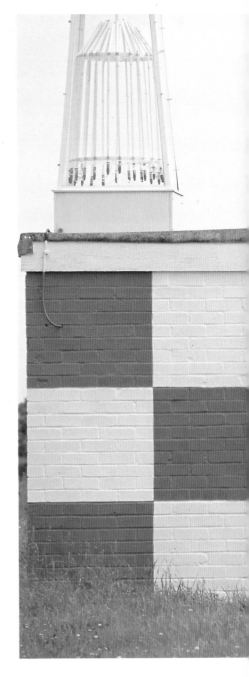

The following photographs were taken for an article comparing the Testarossa and the Robinson R22 helicopter in a commuter challenge on London's orbital nightmare, the M25. Comparing the Testarossa to the Robinson as pure business transportation is, of course, unfair. Would you leave your Ferrari at the mercy of shopping trolleys in a multi storey car park?

The R22 will cruise at 100 mph, unworried by radar guns, VASCAR and the unwanted attentions of the boys in blue. The Ferrari, however, is a good deal more comfortable

waiting list for a Testarossa; when it comes to satisfying demand, Ferrari is driven by passion rather than production volumes.

Robinson, by contrast, is populist. Over 500 R22s will be produced this year, making it the biggest-selling aircraft in the world. And the plan behind it was simple enough. Frank Robinson wanted to do for helicopters what Bill Lear did for executive jets. In 1973, Robinson mortgaged his house and spent six years designing, making and certifying parts for the R22; sometime this autumn, the 2000th Robinson chopper will be produced.

The R22 is light, nimble and ingenious. A de-rated – for reliability from 160bhp to 124bhp, with 131bhp available on take-off – Lycoming piston engine provides reliable power. The Robinson's frame looks a little like a junior race car chassis, with a neat outer skin covering a considerable amount of mechanical ingenuity.

The R22 will cruise at 100mph, unsullied by radar guns, VASCAR and the eagle eye of Plod. You could fly one as high as 14,000ft, but 3000ft will usually suffice for cross-country trips. It has a range of 170 nautical miles. The Ferrari will cruise at 100mph, too, top speed is quoted as 180mph and the Testarossa feels just fine loping along at 140mph. At 15mpg, its 25.3-gallon fuel tanks give a useful range of almost 350 miles.

Working out the actual running costs of the Robinson R22 is much easier than estimating how the Ferrari will hurt your wallet, because the helicopter comes complete with a finite service life: after ten years or 2000 hours aloft, the R22 must be refurbished. A Ferrari Testarossa, on the other hand, can probably look forward to an indefinite life-span, subject to hooking up with an owner who dotes.

Assuming that you can't claim the VAT back, the Robinson stands an owner in at £91,650. Working on a life of 200 hours/year – that is, effectively, around 20,000 miles per annum – the R22 will drink fuel at the rate of £2.97 an hour (around 14.5mpg) and require three services totalling £1,670. Insurance – for the machine and compulsory £1m third-party cover – would cost £3,600.

So, in terms of consumables, the Robinson costs £29.32 an hour, or around 29p a mile. Because of the fixed life-span, basic depreciation is reasonably simple to calculate: the residual value of the machine does depend on the dollar exchange rate and the availability of new R22s at the time when the 2,000 hours are up. Currently a time's-up R22 is worth about £15,000; a £30,000 overhaul will give it a new lease of life.

Depreciation, then, clocks up at £38 an hour when based on the VAT-inclusive price, total running costs per hour work out at approximately £67, giving a total running cost of around 70p per mile.

Buy your Robinson from Mike Wilds at Skyline Helicopters and you get 40 hours of free training, which should be enough to see you licensed and out in the wild blue yonder alone: were you to walk in off the street and demand Skyline provided you with tuition but no helicopter, then the cost of getting you airborne alone would be around £8,000.

You don't need any special training to drive the Testarossa – a standard British driving licence will do nicely, although spending a half-hour on a race-track somewhere would allow you to revel in the deliciously balanced engine without suffering from a case of recurrent blue-light paranoia.

Assessing the depreciation of a Ferrari Testarossa is difficult. A couple of years ago, at the height of the investor-car silliness, a new Testarossa courted a premium as soon as it left the dealer. Today, however, low-mileage cars can be discovered lurking in the small ads of most of the quality Sundays for around £100,000.

According to British Ferrari importer Maranello Concessionaires, few Ferrari Testarossa drivers use their cars for 20,000 miles in 12 months: 'Most cars do between 4000 and 6000 miles a year,' says one spokesman. Assuming that the Testarossa was in good condition, a high-mileage car might be worth 85,000 after a year.

Were a business person to cover 20,000 miles in a Testarossa, then the car would require three services – service intervals are 6,250 miles – and the engine must be removed at 18,750 miles for the replacement of drive-belts. Total service costs, therefore, are £2071.80 + VAT. Add in a road fund licence at £100 and insurance – fully comprehensive for a 35-year-old man living in London who garages his car – at the small price of £3742 per year.

Working on an average of 15mpg – hard driving sees the Testarossa in the 12mpg range, while an 80mph motorway stroll can make the car sip fuel at around 20 mpg – gives a fuel bill of £2733 for the year.

Running a Ferrari Testarossa as a business tool, then, costs around £2.73 per mile, or four times the price of flying a Robinson. The chopper has certain other advantages, too: flying city centre to city centre is easier than driving and you can land the whirlybird pretty well anywhere you have permission.

But, for London-based business flyers, Battersea Heliport, the capital's only public landing pad, is overused. If you go from Battersea to Birmingham's National Exhibition Centre, then the chopper will outrun the Ferrari, thanks to choked city traffic.

Yet travel from Skyline Helicopters' High Wycombe base to Brum, and journey times by car and helicopter are comparable – if the M40 isn't blocked by an accident, a meandering sheep or a Dutch tourist coming over all excited at 58mph in the outside lane. Then again, bad weather can ground the Robinson. Low cloud does not tend to render a Ferrari impotent.

Ultimately, the Robinson R22 is the helicopter made rational and the Ferrari Testarossa is the car made irrational. You could use either as a business implement and be well-pleased with the result: and both vehicles score approximately equal marks on the flashometer, too.

In the end, of course, neither the Robinson nor the Ferrari are business essentials – they are the ultimate business accessory. Which you choose depends on whether the blip-blip noise as you double-declutch the Ferrari or the scything chopper-sound of an R22 going up, up and away makes you smile or grimace. Best of all, you might think, is that the Robinson could eliminate the M25 from your life once and for all. Then again, the Ferrari might just make London's orbital nightmare a road to savour.

Which would you prefer – the swish chop noise of the R22 or the muted growl of the Testarossa?

*Neither machine is as purpose built for
the commuter as a Vauxhall Cavalier*

The Ferrari is certainly more comfortable and has a good deal more luggage space

You'll need 40 hours flying time to qualify to fly the R22, but a normal British driving licence is all you'll need for the Testarossa

Left and below
*Running the Testarossa will cost you
£2.73 per mile, or four times the cost of
the R22*

Right
Getting hold of the R22 is far easier than a Testarossa. There could be anything up to a three-year waiting list for the Ferrari

Left
When all is said and done, the R22 is built for the logical, while the Testarossa is for the illogical

Above and overleaf
In the end of course, neither the Testarossa nor the R22 are business essentials. They are the ultimate business accessories